ALLEN SMITH

Memorizing Psalm 51 - Create in Me a Clean Heart

Memorize Scripture, Memorize the Bible, and Seal God's Word in Your Heart

First published by Nelaco Press 2021

Copyright © 2021 by Allen Smith

All rights reserved. No part of this publication may be reproduced, stored or transmitted in any form or by any means, electronic, mechanical, photocopying, recording, scanning, or otherwise without written permission from the publisher. It is illegal to copy this book, post it to a website, or distribute it by any other means without permission.

Scripture quotations are from The ESV® Bible (The Holy Bible, English Standard Version®), copyright © 2001 by Crossway, a publishing ministry of Good News Publishers. Used by permission. All rights reserved.

First edition

ISBN: 978-1-952381-51-5

This book was professionally typeset on Reedsy.
Find out more at reedsy.com

To my Lord and Savior

Contents

Before You Begin	1
Introduction	2
How To Use This Book	4
Week 1 Prep Work	6
Psalm 51:1	9
Psalm 51:2	11
Psalm 51:3	13
Psalm 51:4	15
Psalm 51:5	17
Psalm 51:6	19
Week 2 Prep Work	22
Psalm 51:7	24
Psalm 51:8	26
Psalm 51:9	28
Psalm 51:10	30
Psalm 51:11	32
Psalm 51:12	34
Week 3 Prep Work	36
Psalm 51:13	38
Psalm 51:14	40
Psalm 51:15	42
Psalm 51:16	44
Psalm 51:17	46
Psalm 51:18	48
Psalm 51:19	50
Conclusion	52

Before You Begin

Hey reader, before you begin memorizing scripture, I wanted to say thank you by offering a free gift.

I wrote a book called Memorize the Sermon on the Mount and I'd like to give you a free copy.

Simply text BIBLE to (678) 506-7543 and I'll send you a free copy straight to your inbox.

I've even thrown in a free bonus gift just for you.

I pray it becomes a blessing to you as you seal God's Word in your heart.

Introduction

I would like to start off by saying that I have prayed for you, whoever you are, wherever you are, as you are just beginning to start this journey to memorize a piece of the Bible.

In this book, you're going to memorize the 51st chapter of the book of Psalm.

In the 51st chapter of the book of Psalm, we hear the heart cry of King David to God. He royally screwed up and now it's all out in the open. In a nutshell, David had an affair with Bathsheba, she got pregnant, he had her husband sent to the front lines of a battle to be killed and hardened his heart from repentance. His sins were great considering he sinned in adultery, murder, and in taking measures to cover his sin. As I said, he royally screwed up.

It seemed like he would get away with it, but we all know nothing is hidden from God. The prophet Nathan was the man God sent to call him out and you can read the entire ordeal in 2 Samuel chapters 11 and 12. After the cat is out of the bag and David feels the full weight of his sins, he comes before God completely broken and honest in Psalm 51.

Though I've never committed murder nor an affair, I've still found myself on several occasions down on my knees broken over my sins. Sins that I've tried to cover up and act as if God couldn't see right through me. There is pain in confession and repentance but there is no peace without it. And through it,

INTRODUCTION

there is forgiveness, mercy, and God's lovingkindness.

Thank goodness we have a merciful God and what better way to continuously be reminded of that fact than by committing this chapter to memory.

That said, Psalm 51 will take some work on your part to commit to memory, but it will absolutely be worth it.

This is a game of repetition over time and this book will guide you every step of the way.

That said, there are no tricks, magic strategies, or brain hacks to make it work.

It just takes work but work that is incredibly rewarding.

But even with all that said, there are probably excuses piling up in your head.

Little lies telling you a thousand reasons why you can't possibly remember a section of the Bible.

"I have a bad memory."

"I don't have enough time."

And many other reasons why you might tell yourself this won't work.

Memorizing a passage of the Bible can feel daunting but you don't need to start off by memorizing everything at once.

You just need to start with one verse.

And with that, you're ready to head to the next chapter to learn how to use this book.

How To Use This Book

By now you are probably curious how this book will work so I will quickly give you an overview.

This book covers the entire 51st chapter of the book of Psalm, English Standard Version.

This passage of scripture is broken down verse by verse and I recommend you memorize one verse each day working your way through memorizing the entire passage.

Each verse has one dedicated chapter and as mentioned before, this book uses the ESV (English Standard Version) translation. You will be guided to either repeat or recite a verse or verses during each chapter.

This book is set up so that you don't need to have your Bible in front of you to read from.

There are a handful of chapters, though optional, that are the weekly preparation chapters involving some optional prep work. This prep work will make memorizing the entire passage significantly easier and time well spent on your journey to memorizing God's Word. I highly recommend you do it, but feel free to skip it.

HOW TO USE THIS BOOK

Also, I do not require you to say the verse number when memorizing scripture. The original scriptures were not numbered into verses so I don't believe that is a critical piece to remember. However, if you would like to state the verse number when reciting each verse, you are more than welcome to.

As you work your way through memorizing each verse, there will be days where you will get frustrated. It will seem the verse just won't stick. That is completely normal. Some verses will be significantly harder to memorize than others. That is okay. Don't be afraid to repeat a chapter if you feel you didn't quite memorize the verse that day.

If the first round of repetition didn't help it stick, the second or third round should surely do the trick.

You are ready to begin on a wonderful, spirit-filled journey to solidifying a piece of God's Word inside of your heart.

May it be an incredible blessing on your life and your personal walk with Christ.

Week 1 Prep Work

Welcome to the preparation work on your journey to memorizing Psalm 51.

Like I mentioned in the introduction, this work is completely optional, but I cannot encourage you enough to do the prep work.

If you had four hours to chop down a tree with a dull axe, you would be better off sharpening your axe for two of those four hours before getting started.

This prep work is sharpening your axe.

It will make everything moving forward significantly easier.

Though it will take time, this will be time well spent which you may not realize until you begin memorizing each verse one by one.

To complete the prep work, you will need to read the passage out loud 50 times.

Sounds daunting, doesn't it?

Reading out loud Psalm 51 would take roughly 2 and half minutes. Do that 50 times and you are looking at roughly 2 hours worth of reading out loud.

Not many people would have the luxury in spare time to squeeze that in and

WEEK 1 PREP WORK

I'm not asking you to.

Instead of doing the entire passage in one go, you are going to do a smaller chunk that would allow you to accomplish the task in an hour or less.

You are going to focus on just the first six verses as you read them out loud 50 times.

Don't have an hour?

Do it for 30 minutes running through them 25 times.

Or commit to what you can. I assure you, whatever you do here will help.

Whenever you try to memorize something from scratch, it can feel like there is a lot of resistance to get the material to stick in your brain.

But if you are very familiar with whatever you are trying to commit to memory, it is like globbing memory glue on it before you get started.

After each week, you will have an opportunity to attempt the next block of 6 verses for the following week.

If you have decided to do the prep work, get ready to read the following chunk of verses out loud. Oh, and grab a glass of water. Your mouth can get pretty dry doing this prep work.

Please note, I left the verse numbers in the passage on the next page for your reference only.

When you are ready, begin.

MEMORIZING PSALM 51 - CREATE IN ME A CLEAN HEART

1 Have mercy on me, O God, according to your steadfast love; according to your abundant mercy blot out my transgressions. 2 Wash me thoroughly from my iniquity, and cleanse me from my sin! 3 For I know my transgressions, and my sin is ever before me. 4 Against you, you only, have I sinned and done what is evil in your sight, so that you may be justified in your words and blameless in your judgment. 5 Behold, I was brought forth in iniquity, and in sin did my mother conceive me. 6 Behold, you delight in truth in the inward being, and you teach me wisdom in the secret heart. (Psalm 51:1-6 ESV)

See you tomorrow!

Psalm 51:1

Today you are going to memorize Psalm 51:1.

You are going to memorize the verse by using the 10-10-10 method.

To use this method, each verse will be repeated out loud 10 times and then immediately recited 10 times from memory. In later chapters, you'll start combining verses and reciting those 10 times as well.

Don't worry if that was a little confusing to follow. Just follow the instructions and you will do just fine.

I understand 10 times may seem excessive and tedious, but trust me, this is necessary. There will be times where it may take you speaking a verse 5 times or more just to fully nail it down before being able to recite it from memory.

As a last word of advice before you begin, I wanted to share with you a few tips that have helped me memorize scripture:

1. Speaking the verse with conviction or emotion as you repeat or recite it from memory.
2. Emphasizing a different word each time you say it out loud.
3. Use hand motions as you speak.
4. Creating images in your head corresponding to each piece of a verse.

5. Singing a verse or a piece of a verse instead of speaking it.

Yes, you heard that last one right. It's weird, it works, but don't feel you need to incorporate all of these at once or any at all. As you go deeper into memorizing scripture, you will find what works for you and what doesn't.

Let's begin.

Say the following verse out loud ten times. You do not have to say the citation within the parenthesis.

"Have mercy on me, O God, according to your steadfast love; according to your abundant mercy blot out my transgressions" (Psalm 51:1).

When you are done, recite the verse ten times in a row from memory, doing your best not to look at the verse.

Great job! You got your first verse down!

Throughout your day when you are driving your car, taking a break from work, or cooking a meal, go over what you've memorized so far to keep reinforcing it in your mind.

Tomorrow you'll quickly review what you learned today and add another verse to it.

If you don't feel confident you've truly memorized today's verse, consider going through the chapter again.

See you tomorrow!

God Bless.

Psalm 51:2

Today you are going to memorize Psalm 51:2.

After you review what you have already learned, you are going to memorize today's verse using the 10-10-10 Method.

Let's begin.

Let's review the verse you learned yesterday by reciting it 10 times from memory. Glance over it if you need a refresher.

"Have mercy on me, O God, according to your steadfast love; according to your abundant mercy blot out my transgressions" (Psalm 51:1).

When your review is done, let's get into today's verse.

Say the following verse out loud 10 times.

"Wash me thoroughly from my iniquity, and cleanse me from my sin!" (Psalm 51:2).

When you are done, recite the verse 10 times in a row from memory, doing your best not to look at the verse.

MEMORIZING PSALM 51 - CREATE IN ME A CLEAN HEART

Great job! You got your next verse down!

You know the drill. Throughout your day when you're driving to work, taking a break from work, or cooking a meal, go over what you've memorized so far to keep reinforcing it in your mind.

Tomorrow you'll quickly review what you learned today and add another verse to it.

If you don't feel confident you've truly memorized today's verse, consider listening through the chapter again.

See you tomorrow!

Good Bless

Psalm 51:3

Today you are going to memorize Psalm 51:3.

After you review what you have already learned, you are going to memorize today's verse using the 10-10-10 Method.

Let's begin.

Let's review the verse you learned yesterday by reciting it 10 times from memory. Glance over it if you need a refresher.

"Wash me thoroughly from my iniquity, and cleanse me from my sin!" (Psalm 51:2).

Now you're going to review all the verses you have memorized up to this point by reciting them 10 times. You can find it in the prep work chapter for this week if you need a refresher. If after three times you feel confident in your ability to recite all the verses you have currently memorized, feel free to call it good enough.

When your review is done, let's get into today's verse.

Say the following verse out loud 10 times:

MEMORIZING PSALM 51 - CREATE IN ME A CLEAN HEART

"For I know my transgressions, and my sin is ever before me" (Psalm 51:3).

When you are done, recite the verse 10 times in a row from memory, doing your best not to look at the verse.

Great job! You got your next verse down!

You know the drill, throughout your day when you're driving to work, taking a break from work, or cooking a meal, go over what you've memorized so far to keep reinforcing it in your mind.

Tomorrow you'll quickly review what you learned today and add another verse to it.

If you don't feel confident you've truly memorized today's verse, consider listening through the chapter again.

See you tomorrow!

God bless.

Psalm 51:4

Today you are going to memorize Psalm 51:4.

After you review what you have already learned, you are going to memorize today's verse using the 10-10-10 Method.

Let's begin.

Let's review the verse you learned yesterday by reciting it 10 times from memory. Glance over it if you need a refresher.

"For I know my transgressions, and my sin is ever before me" (Psalm 51:3).

Now you're going to review all the verses you have memorized up to this point by reciting them 10 times. You can find it in the prep work chapter for this week if you need a refresher. If after three times you feel confident in your ability to recite all the verses you have currently memorized, feel free to call it good enough.

When your review is done, let's get into today's verse.

Say the following verse out loud 10 times:

"Against you, you only, have I sinned and done what is evil in your sight, so

that you may be justified in your words and blameless in your judgment" (Psalm 51:4).

When you are done, recite the verse 10 times in a row from memory, doing your best not to look at the verse.

Great job! You got your next verse down!

You know the drill, throughout your day when you're driving to work, taking a break from work, or cooking a meal, go over what you've memorized so far to keep reinforcing it in your mind.

Tomorrow you'll quickly review what you learned today and add another verse to it.

If you don't feel confident you've truly memorized today's verse, consider listening through the chapter again.

See you tomorrow!
 God bless.

Psalm 51:5

Today you are going to memorize Psalm 51:5.

After you review what you have already learned, you are going to memorize today's verse using the 10-10-10 Method.

Let's begin.

Let's review the verse you learned yesterday by reciting it 10 times from memory. Glance over it if you need a refresher.

"Against you, you only, have I sinned and done what is evil in your sight, so that you may be justified in your words and blameless in your judgment" (Psalm 51:4).

Now you're going to review all the verses you have memorized up to this point by reciting them 10 times. You can find it in the prep work chapter for this week if you need a refresher. If after three times you feel confident in your ability to recite all the verses you have currently memorized, feel free to call it good enough.

When your review is done, let's get into today's verse.

Say the following verse out loud 10 times:

"Behold, I was brought forth in iniquity, and in sin did my mother conceive me" (Psalm 51:5).

When you are done, recite the verse 10 times in a row from memory, doing your best not to look at the verse.

Great job! You got your next verse down!

You know the drill, throughout your day when you're driving to work, taking a break from work, or cooking a meal, go over what you've memorized so far to keep reinforcing it in your mind.

Tomorrow you'll quickly review what you learned today and add another verse to it.

If you don't feel confident you've truly memorized today's verse, consider listening through the chapter again.

See you tomorrow!

God bless.

Psalm 51:6

Today you are going to memorize Psalm 51:6.

After you review what you have already learned, you are going to memorize today's verse using the 10-10-10 Method.

Let's begin.

Let's review the verse you learned yesterday by reciting it 10 times from memory. Glance over it if you need a refresher.

"Behold, I was brought forth in iniquity, and in sin did my mother conceive me" (Psalm 51:5).

Now you're going to review all the verses you have memorized up to this point by reciting them 10 times. You can find it in the prep work chapter for this week if you need a refresher. If after three times you feel confident in your ability to recite all the verses you have currently memorized, feel free to call it good enough.

When your review is done, let's get into today's verse.

Say the following verse out loud 10 times:

"Behold, you delight in truth in the inward being, and you teach me wisdom in the secret heart" (Psalm 51:6).

When you are done, recite the verse 10 times in a row from memory, doing your best not to look at the verse.

Great job! You got your next verse down and your first block of 6 verses, too!

With your first block of verses completed, I would love to hear what you think so far about the book in the form of a review.

Reviews help other listeners find this book so that they too can become more intimate with God's Word.

Better yet, leaving a review is easy.

Simply go to the book's page on Amazon, scroll down and click the 'leave a customer review' button, choose a rating, leave a few words, and you're done!

Bonus points for leaving a picture with your review.

Super bonus points for a video.

Just a few minutes of your time will help people from all over the world, people you may never meet in this life, find this book and seal God's Word in their hearts.

Tomorrow you have the optional prep work for the next block of 6 verses. Though it's not mandatory, I can't stress enough how beneficial it will be moving forward.

If you plan to skip it, simply move to the following chapter to begin memorizing the first verse of the next block of 6 verses.

PSALM 51:6

See you tomorrow!

God Bless!

Week 2 Prep Work

If you are here, that tells me you are ready for your next block of verses to memorize.

Great job so far. I know it takes a lot of time and effort to memorize scripture and I hope all that time and effort has been a joyful experience.

Just like with the first round of prep work, this is completely optional.

You are not required to do this to memorize the next block of 6 verses.

But like I said before, it will make the task much easier.

If you are not up for the prep work, feel free to skip this chapter.

If you are willing to give it a shot, get ready to read the next 6 verses out loud 50 times which will take you about an hour.

If you don't have an hour, run through them 25 times which will only take you about 30 minutes.

Or commit to whatever you can.

Anything and everything you do here will help moving forward.

WEEK 2 PREP WORK

Please note, I left the verse numbers in the passage for your reference only.

When you are ready, begin.

7 Purge me with hyssop, and I shall be clean; wash me, and I shall be whiter than snow. 8 Let me hear joy and gladness; let the bones that you have broken rejoice. 9 Hide your face from my sins, and blot out all my iniquities. 10 Create in me a clean heart, O God, and renew a right spirit within me. 11 Cast me not away from your presence, and take not your Holy Spirit from me. 12 Restore to me the joy of your salvation, and uphold me with a willing spirit. (Psalm 51:7-12)

See you tomorrow!

Psalm 51:7

Today you are going to memorize Psalm 51:7.

After you review what you have already learned, you are going to memorize today's verse using the 10-10-10 Method.

Let's begin.

Let's review the verse you learned last by reciting it 10 times from memory. Glance over it if you need a refresher.

"Behold, you delight in truth in the inward being, and you teach me wisdom in the secret heart" (Psalm 51:6).

Now you're going to review all the verses you have memorized up to this point by reciting them 10 times. You can find it in the prep work chapter for this week if you need a refresher. If after three times you feel confident in your ability to recite all the verses you have currently memorized, feel free to call it good enough.

When your review is done, let's get into today's verse.

Say the following verse out loud 10 times:

"Purge me with hyssop, and I shall be clean; wash me, and I shall be whiter than snow" (Psalm 51:7).

When you are done, recite the verse 10 times in a row from memory, doing your best not to look at the verse.

Great job! You got your next verse down!

You know the drill, throughout your day when you're driving to work, taking a break from work, or cooking a meal, go over what you've memorized so far to keep reinforcing it in your mind.

Tomorrow you'll quickly review what you learned today and add another verse to it.

If you don't feel confident you've truly memorized today's verse, consider listening through the chapter again.

See you tomorrow!

God bless.

Psalm 51:8

Today you are going to memorize Psalm 51:8.

After you review what you have already learned, you are going to memorize today's verse using the 10-10-10 Method.

Let's begin.

Let's review the verse you learned yesterday by reciting it 10 times from memory. Glance over it if you need a refresher.

"Purge me with hyssop, and I shall be clean; wash me, and I shall be whiter than snow" (Psalm 51:7).

Now you're going to review all the verses you have memorized up to this point by reciting them 10 times. You can find it in the prep work chapter for this week if you need a refresher. If after three times you feel confident in your ability to recite all the verses you have currently memorized, feel free to call it good enough.

When your review is done, let's get into today's verse.

Say the following verse out loud 10 times:

"Let me hear joy and gladness; let the bones that you have broken rejoice" (Psalm 51:8).

When you are done, recite the verse 10 times in a row from memory, doing your best not to look at the verse.

Great job! You got your next verse down!

You know the drill, throughout your day when you're driving to work, taking a break from work, or cooking a meal, go over what you've memorized so far to keep reinforcing it in your mind.

Tomorrow you'll quickly review what you learned today and add another verse to it.

If you don't feel confident you've truly memorized today's verse, consider listening through the chapter again.

See you tomorrow!

God bless.

Psalm 51:9

Today you are going to memorize Psalm 51:9.

After you review what you have already learned, you are going to memorize today's verse using the 10-10-10 Method.

Let's begin.

Let's review the verse you learned yesterday by reciting it 10 times from memory. Glance over it if you need a refresher.

"Let me hear joy and gladness; let the bones that you have broken rejoice" (Psalm 51:8).

Now you're going to review all the verses you have memorized up to this point by reciting them 10 times. You can find it in the prep work chapter for this week if you need a refresher. If after three times you feel confident in your ability to recite all the verses you have currently memorized, feel free to call it good enough.

When your review is done, let's get into today's verse.

Say the following verse out loud 10 times:

"Hide your face from my sins, and blot out all my iniquities" (Psalm 51:9).

When you are done, recite the verse 10 times in a row from memory, doing your best not to look at the verse.

Great job! You got your next verse down!

You know the drill, throughout your day when you're driving to work, taking a break from work, or cooking a meal, go over what you've memorized so far to keep reinforcing it in your mind.

Tomorrow you'll quickly review what you learned today and add another verse to it.

If you don't feel confident you've truly memorized today's verse, consider listening through the chapter again.

See you tomorrow!

God bless.

Psalm 51:10

Today you are going to memorize Psalm 51:10.

After you review what you have already learned, you are going to memorize today's verse using the 10-10-10 Method.

Let's begin.

Let's review the verse you learned yesterday by reciting it 10 times from memory. Glance over it if you need a refresher.

"Hide your face from my sins, and blot out all my iniquities" (Psalm 51:9).

Now you're going to review all the verses you have memorized up to this point by reciting them 10 times. You can find it in the prep work chapter for this week if you need a refresher. If after three times you feel confident in your ability to recite all the verses you have currently memorized, feel free to call it good enough.

When your review is done, let's get into today's verse.

Say the following verse out loud 10 times:

"Create in me a clean heart, O God, and renew a right spirit within me"

(Psalm 51:10).

When you are done, recite the verse 10 times in a row from memory, doing your best not to look at the verse.

Great job! You got your next verse down!

You know the drill, throughout your day when you're driving to work, taking a break from work, or cooking a meal, go over what you've memorized so far to keep reinforcing it in your mind.

Tomorrow you'll quickly review what you learned today and add another verse to it.

If you don't feel confident you've truly memorized today's verse, consider listening through the chapter again.

See you tomorrow!

God bless.

Psalm 51:11

Today you are going to memorize Psalm 51:11.

After you review what you have already learned, you are going to memorize today's verse using the 10-10-10 Method.

Let's begin.

Let's review the verse you learned yesterday by reciting it 10 times from memory. Glance over it if you need a refresher.

"Create in me a clean heart, O God, and renew a right spirit within me" (Psalm 51:10).

Now you're going to review all the verses you have memorized up to this point by reciting them 10 times. You can find it in the prep work chapter for this week if you need a refresher. If after three times you feel confident in your ability to recite all the verses you have currently memorized, feel free to call it good enough.

When your review is done, let's get into today's verse.

Say the following verse out loud 10 times:

"Cast me not away from your presence, and take not your Holy Spirit from me" (Psalm 51:11).

When you are done, recite the verse 10 times in a row from memory, doing your best not to look at the verse.

Great job! You got your next verse down!

You know the drill, throughout your day when you're driving to work, taking a break from work, or cooking a meal, go over what you've memorized so far to keep reinforcing it in your mind.

Tomorrow you'll quickly review what you learned today and add another verse to it.

If you don't feel confident you've truly memorized today's verse, consider listening through the chapter again.

See you tomorrow!

God bless.

Psalm 51:12

Today you are going to memorize Psalm 51:12.

After you review what you have already learned, you are going to memorize today's verse using the 10-10-10 Method.

Let's begin.

Let's review the verse you learned yesterday by reciting it 10 times from memory. Glance over it if you need a refresher.

"Cast me not away from your presence, and take not your Holy Spirit from me" (Psalm 51:11).

Now you're going to review all the verses you have memorized up to this point by reciting them 10 times. You can find it in the prep work chapter for this week if you need a refresher. If after three times you feel confident in your ability to recite all the verses you have currently memorized, feel free to call it good enough.

When your review is done, let's get into today's verse.

Say the following verse out loud 10 times:

"Restore to me the joy of your salvation, and uphold me with a willing spirit" (Psalm 51:12).

When you are done, recite the verse 10 times in a row from memory, doing your best not to look at the verse.

Great job! You got your next verse down!

You know the drill, throughout your day when you're driving to work, taking a break from work, or cooking a meal, go over what you've memorized so far to keep reinforcing it in your mind.

Tomorrow you have the optional prep work for the last block of 7 verses. Though it's not mandatory, I can't stress enough how beneficial it will be moving forward.

If you plan to skip it, simply move to the following chapter to begin memorizing the first verse of the last block of 7 verses.

If you don't feel confident you've truly memorized today's verse, consider listening through the chapter again.

See you tomorrow!

God bless.

Week 3 Prep Work

If you are here, that tells me you are ready for your last block of verses to memorize.

Great job so far. I know it takes a lot of time and effort to memorize scripture and I hope all that time and effort has been a joyful experience.

Just like with the first round of prep work, this is completely optional.

You are not required to do this to memorize the last block of 7 verses.

But like I said before, it will make the task much easier.

If you are not up for the prep work, feel free to skip this chapter.

If you are willing to give it a shot, get ready to read the last 7 verses out loud 50 times which will take you about an hour.

If you don't have an hour, run through them 25 times which will only take you about 30 minutes.

Or commit to whatever you can.

Anything and everything you do here will help moving forward.

Please note, I left the verse numbers in the passage for your reference only.

When you are ready, begin.

13 Then I will teach transgressors your ways, and sinners will return to you. 14 Deliver me from bloodguiltiness, O God, O God of my salvation, and my tongue will sing aloud of your righteousness. 15 O Lord, open my lips, and my mouth will declare your praise. 16 For you will not delight in sacrifice, or I would give it; you will not be pleased with a burnt offering. 17 The sacrifices of God are a broken spirit; a broken and contrite heart, O God, you will not despise. 18 Do good to Zion in your good pleasure; build up the walls of Jerusalem; 19 then will you delight in right sacrifices, in burnt offerings and whole burnt offerings; then bulls will be offered on your altar. (Psalm 51:13-19)

See you tomorrow!

Psalm 51:13

Today you are going to memorize Psalm 51:13.

After you review what you have already learned, you are going to memorize today's verse using the 10-10-10 Method.

Let's begin.

Let's review the verse you learned yesterday by reciting it 10 times from memory. Glance over it if you need a refresher.

"Restore to me the joy of your salvation, and uphold me with a willing spirit" (Psalm 51:12).

Now you're going to review all the verses you have memorized up to this point by reciting them 10 times. You can find it in the prep work chapter for this week if you need a refresher. If after three times you feel confident in your ability to recite all the verses you have currently memorized, feel free to call it good enough.

When your review is done, let's get into today's verse.

Say the following verse out loud 10 times:

"Then I will teach transgressors your ways, and sinners will return to you" (Psalm 51:13).

When you are done, recite the verse 10 times in a row from memory, doing your best not to look at the verse.

Great job! You got your next verse down!

You know the drill, throughout your day when you're driving to work, taking a break from work, or cooking a meal, go over what you've memorized so far to keep reinforcing it in your mind.

Tomorrow you'll quickly review what you learned today and add another verse to it.

If you don't feel confident you've truly memorized today's verse, consider listening through the chapter again.

See you tomorrow!

God bless.

Psalm 51:14

Today you are going to memorize Psalm 51:14.

After you review what you have already learned, you are going to memorize today's verse using the 10-10-10 Method.

Let's begin.

Let's review the verse you learned last by reciting it 10 times from memory. Glance over it if you need a refresher.

"Then I will teach transgressors your ways, and sinners will return to you" (Psalm 51:13).

Now you're going to review all the verses you have memorized up to this point by reciting them 10 times. You can find it in the prep work chapter for this week if you need a refresher. If after three times you feel confident in your ability to recite all the verses you have currently memorized, feel free to call it good enough.

When your review is done, let's get into today's verse.

Say the following verse out loud 10 times:

"Deliver me from bloodguiltiness, O God, O God of my salvation, and my tongue will sing aloud of your righteousness" (Psalm 51:14).

When you are done, recite the verse 10 times in a row from memory, doing your best not to look at the verse.

Great job! You got your next verse down!

You know the drill, throughout your day when you're driving to work, taking a break from work, or cooking a meal, go over what you've memorized so far to keep reinforcing it in your mind.

Tomorrow you'll quickly review what you learned today and add another verse to it.

If you don't feel confident you've truly memorized today's verse, consider listening through the chapter again.

See you tomorrow!

God bless.

Psalm 51:15

Today you are going to memorize Psalm 51:15.

After you review what you have already learned, you are going to memorize today's verse using the 10-10-10 Method.

Let's begin.

Let's review the verse you learned yesterday by reciting it 10 times from memory. Glance over it if you need a refresher.

"Deliver me from bloodguiltiness, O God, O God of my salvation, and my tongue will sing aloud of your righteousness" (Psalm 51:14).

Now you're going to review all the verses you have memorized up to this point by reciting them 10 times. You can find it in the prep work chapter for this week if you need a refresher. If after three times you feel confident in your ability to recite all the verses you have currently memorized, feel free to call it good enough.

When your review is done, let's get into today's verse.

Say the following verse out loud 10 times:

"O Lord, open my lips, and my mouth will declare your praise" (Psalm 51:15).

When you are done, recite the verse 10 times in a row from memory, doing your best not to look at the verse.

Great job! You got your next verse down!

You know the drill, throughout your day when you're driving to work, taking a break from work, or cooking a meal, go over what you've memorized so far to keep reinforcing it in your mind.

Tomorrow you'll quickly review what you learned today and add another verse to it.

If you don't feel confident you've truly memorized today's verse, consider listening through the chapter again.

See you tomorrow!

God bless.

Psalm 51:16

Today you are going to memorize Psalm 51:16.

After you review what you have already learned, you are going to memorize today's verse using the 10-10-10 Method.

Let's begin.

Let's review the verse you learned yesterday by reciting it 10 times from memory. Glance over it if you need a refresher.

"O Lord, open my lips, and my mouth will declare your praise" (Psalm 51:15).

Now you're going to review all the verses you have memorized up to this point by reciting them 10 times. You can find it in the prep work chapter for this week if you need a refresher. If after three times you feel confident in your ability to recite all the verses you have currently memorized, feel free to call it good enough.

When your review is done, let's get into today's verse.

Say the following verse out loud 10 times:

"For you will not delight in sacrifice, or I would give it; you will not be pleased with a burnt offering" (Psalm 51:16).

When you are done, recite the verse 10 times in a row from memory, doing your best not to look at the verse.

Great job! You got your next verse down!

You know the drill, throughout your day when you're driving to work, taking a break from work, or cooking a meal, go over what you've memorized so far to keep reinforcing it in your mind.

Tomorrow you'll quickly review what you learned today and add another verse to it.

If you don't feel confident you've truly memorized today's verse, consider listening through the chapter again.

See you tomorrow!

God bless.

Psalm 51:17

Today you are going to memorize Psalm 51:17.

After you review what you have already learned, you are going to memorize today's verse using the 10-10-10 Method.

Let's begin.

Let's review the verse you learned yesterday by reciting it 10 times from memory. Glance over it if you need a refresher.

"For you will not delight in sacrifice, or I would give it; you will not be pleased with a burnt offering" (Psalm 51:16).

Now you're going to review all the verses you have memorized up to this point by reciting them 10 times. You can find it in the prep work chapter for this week if you need a refresher. If after three times you feel confident in your ability to recite all the verses you have currently memorized, feel free to call it good enough.

When your review is done, let's get into today's verse.

Say the following verse out loud 10 times:

"The sacrifices of God are a broken spirit; a broken and contrite heart, O God, you will not despise" (Psalm 51:17).

When you are done, recite the verse 10 times in a row from memory, doing your best not to look at the verse.

Great job! You got your next verse down!

You know the drill, throughout your day when you're driving to work, taking a break from work, or cooking a meal, go over what you've memorized so far to keep reinforcing it in your mind.

Tomorrow you'll quickly review what you learned today and add another verse to it.

If you don't feel confident you've truly memorized today's verse, consider listening through the chapter again.

See you tomorrow!

God bless.

Psalm 51:18

Today you are going to memorize Psalm 51:18.

After you review what you have already learned, you are going to memorize today's verse using the 10-10-10 Method.

Let's begin.

Let's review the verse you learned yesterday by reciting it 10 times from memory. Glance over it if you need a refresher.

"The sacrifices of God are a broken spirit; a broken and contrite heart, O God, you will not despise" (Psalm 51:17).

Now you're going to review all the verses you have memorized up to this point by reciting them 10 times. You can find it in the prep work chapter for this week if you need a refresher. If after three times you feel confident in your ability to recite all the verses you have currently memorized, feel free to call it good enough.

When your review is done, let's get into today's verse.

Say the following verse out loud 10 times:

"Do good to Zion in your good pleasure; build up the walls of Jerusalem" (Psalm 51:18).

When you are done, recite the verse 10 times in a row from memory, doing your best not to look at the verse.

Great job! You got your next verse down!

You know the drill, throughout your day when you're driving to work, taking a break from work, or cooking a meal, go over what you've memorized so far to keep reinforcing it in your mind.

Tomorrow you'll quickly review what you learned today and add another verse to it.

If you don't feel confident you've truly memorized today's verse, consider listening through the chapter again.

See you tomorrow!

God bless.

Psalm 51:19

Today you are going to memorize Psalm 51:19.

After you review what you have already learned, you are going to memorize today's verse using the 10-10-10 Method.

Let's begin.

Let's review the verse you learned yesterday by reciting it 10 times from memory. Glance over it if you need a refresher.

"Do good to Zion in your good pleasure; build up the walls of Jerusalem" (Psalm 51:18).

Now you're going to review all the verses you have memorized up to this point by reciting them 10 times. You can find it in the prep work chapter for this week if you need a refresher. If after three times you feel confident in your ability to recite all the verses you have currently memorized, feel free to call it good enough.

When your review is done, let's get into today's verse.

Say the following verse out loud 10 times:

"Then will you delight in right sacrifices, in burnt offerings and whole burnt offerings; then bulls will be offered on your altar" (Psalm 51:19).

When you are done, recite the verse 10 times in a row from memory, doing your best not to look at the verse.

Great job! You got your last verse down!

You know the drill, throughout your day when you're driving to work, taking a break from work, or cooking a meal, go over what you've memorized so far to keep reinforcing it in your mind.

If you don't feel confident you've truly memorized today's verse, consider listening through the chapter again.

God bless.

Conclusion

If you are here, I hope that means you have fully memorized the 51st chapter of the book of Psalm.

I hope the experience was rewarding and enriching as you sealed part of God's Word in your heart.

I recommend reciting the full passage every day for the next 30 days to truly solidify that piece of scripture in your mind.

Once you're done, consider memorizing another passage or even an entire book of the Bible!

Lastly, if you have enjoyed this book, do consider leaving a review. I look forward to seeing your feedback.

May God bless you on your journey to further know Him, and I leave you with these two verses, "All Scripture is breathed out by God and profitable for teaching, for reproof, for correction, and for training in righteousness, that the man of God may be complete, equipped for every good work" (2 Timothy 3:16-17).

www.ingramcontent.com/pod-product-compliance
Lightning Source LLC
Chambersburg PA
CBHW030139100526
44592CB00011B/966